BONEY-FINGERED REACH FOR GOD

BONEY-FINGERED REACH FOR GOD

Poems by
Mark Russell Brown

Accents Publishing • Lexington, Kentucky • 2023

Copyright © 2023 by Mark Russell Brown
All rights reserved

Printed in the United States of America

Accents Publishing
Editor: Katerina Stoykova
Cover Photo by Carson Greenhalgh on *Unsplash*

Library of Congress Control Number: 2023936484
ISBN: 978-1-936628-99-5
First Edition

Accents Publishing is an independent press for brilliant voices. For a catalog of current and upcoming titles, please visit us on the Web at

www.accents-publishing.com

CONTENTS

Foreword / vii

I

A Sense of Misplace / 3
Why I Left the Garden / 4
Pieta April 1965 / 5
Miss Bloom / 6
Summers With Danny and Susan / 8
The Swells of Summer / 9
Teacher's Pet / 11
Libby's Kiss / 12
Making It Perfect for the Barge Man / 13
Make Love With War / 14
The Day Dad Died / 15

II

Kissing the Ugly / 19
Effie May's Confession / 20
Evil Iago, Who Is Seen Eavesdropping at the Left / 21
The Blues Are Someone Else's Paper Cut / 22
While at Frisch's for a Tuna Melt / 23
Thirty-Nine for Hot Sizzle / 24

III

Breakfast of Solomon / 27
What Lingers When Lips Part / 28
Atlas Elegy / 29
Sailors Take Warning / 30
Five Years Later / 31
May Day / 32

IV

Until the Resurrection / 35
A Fat Gold Watch / 36
All This and Heaven, Too / 37

Reliquary Sonnet / 38
St. Joseph Speaks / 39
Tower of Babel / 40
How Blake Ruined My Sleep / 41

V

Anima Comes Ashore / 45
Anima Laments the Possibility of Seed / 47
Anima Comments on One Night Stands / 48
Anima Comments on Marriage / 50
Anima's Headache / 51

VI

Prologue: Ode to Prometheus / 55
Irene's Lullaby for a Dying Light / 56
Dracula Courts His Next Ex-Wife / 57
Miss Curie Regrets She's Unable to Lunch Today, Madame / 58
The Ex-Wife of Dracula Counts Her Losses. / 59
The Ex-Wife of Dracula Worries and Lies Awake / 61
The Ex-Wife of Dracula Unfeels / 63
The Count Takes His Waking Slow / 64
Ex-Wife of Dracula Struggles With Indecision / 65

Acknowledgments / 67
About the Author / 69

FOREWORD

Mark Brown appeared one first Saturday of the month, not sure what year or what month, on a couch in the home of one of us mainly women of Green River Writers—mainly older women; I was one of two regulars under 50. Mark was a jocular, sweet, bespectacled teddy bear of a man, and at the time of that first encounter, I recognized him as a brother—oh yes, a brother by another mother, but certainly kin—well of course he charmed everyone in Green River, and we were all in awe of his talent; I don't know who coined the moniker *The Poetry God*, but it stuck.

Fast forward to 2011. I had probably known Mark a good twelve years. We had entered the Spalding University Brief Residency MFA in Writing program at the same time and both taken an Enrichment semester, so we both graduated in November of 2006. After that, he would come over frequently for home-cooked meals (he otherwise had a propensity for ordering pizza in) and often to help me and my then partner Rae with our computers, for he was gifted in high tech. The last Wednesday he came he seemed distracted and like he wasn't quite satisfied when he left. I couldn't reach him by phone the following week, so I sent out an inquiry to his other friends and received the devastating response from his friend Rebecca: "Mark has passed away." I stared dumbly at those horrible words forever before calling Rae over.

His funeral in Cloverport, Kentucky was beautiful and well attended. His sister Rachel tearfully read his signature poem, "A Sense of Misplace," with the opening stanza that sticks in my mind: "Rural Kentucky plus gay equals / ache of never feeling planted." Mark took his own life. He may never have realized how well loved he was.

But lest one think of Mark Russell Brown as a person who was always morose, let us look at some other snippets of his poetry: "I'm helium high / bounce on life's big belly / fat with laughter / the good times taste like Christmas candy / friends at the door whenever it's opened / I'm not alone or blue." This from a poem cleverly titled "The Blues Are Someone Else's Paper Cut."

Yes, in the collection *Boney-Fingered Reach For God*, Mark writes of the loss of his brother and father, about lost love, and yes that "ache" of being gay, but he also writes about the joy of gay sex, for example in "Breakfast of Solomon": "In this morning / of us, you splay like a biscuit for me / and lie prepared as I flow over you, / sawmill gravy, into every crevice."

But Mark's book reaches perhaps its creative pinnacle toward the end when he wows us with the poems about Dracula's ex-wife, the idea being, this person is Nobel Prize winner Madame Curie.

From "The Ex-Wife of Dracula Worries and Lies Awake": "Have you been eating sheep / again? Babies? Your hunger / unsettles my repose. Transfuses / it with cries and bleats. / I have seen you gnaw / on angel bones"

I miss my fabulous, humorous, boisterous, dazzlingly creative friend/ brother Mark, the only person I've been drunk with (twice) in the past 30 years, but now the world is fortunate indeed, for his work will see the light of day, a thing I've hoped for chronically. I am grateful to Katya Stoykova of Accents Publishing for quickly realizing the poems are awesome; Mark was a craftsman; there is nothing sloppy in these poems, which he worked at with grit and determination—he just never wanted to fail, once the idea for a poem was germinating in him. I want to thank Spalding and Green River Writers for both gave Mark venues and platforms to shine in, and some of his happiest moments. Thank you, Mark; your life was way too short, but you gave me gifts to last me forever. It seems appropriate to say, "Amen."

—Harriet Leach

For
My sister, Rachel Crist
& My brothers Frank Isom, Don, and Mike Brown
In Honor of my mother, Mildred J. Brown
In Memory of my father, Russell L. Brown
& my brother, Philip E. Brown
With Special Gratitude for my brother-in-law, Roger Crist

I

A SENSE OF MISPLACE

Rural Kentucky plus gay equals
ache of never feeling planted

when all around you
are rows and rows

of tobacco rooted
so deep it can't be pulled.

I couldn't tap
this soil for pabulum

or grip the clods
that others held tight.

I never conjured
the magic of plunging

gnarled fingers
into this hard clay.

I was the anti-farmer,
the odd non-member,

the alfalfa sprout that flaunted
its clean, blanched root

obscenely in the air.

WHY I LEFT THE GARDEN

One sad childhood, I learned a brother
cannot die and be forgotten

while his roots still grip
underneath, dead hairs that tear

moisture from the surviving
shoots. Like a sickly sprout

beneath a tarp that lay all
June on the lawn, I grew

bent and pale, a crab among blue
grass. In the dapple of the family tree,

I trellised myself and tendrilled
for miles, trying to escape his shade,

but in the scraps of sun I saw
that I carry him with me

like a snail shell. The sluggy
death I thought I left back there

is here and here and here.

PIETA APRIL 1965

Her face drawn tight
like Giotto's lamenting angels,

wings enfold her breast for warmth.
Turned mourning dove, she built

her nest in a distant grotto
to brood an egg

that wicked away her heat, to cradle
a heart that held no beat, while we were left

to rock the throbbing of our own.
                    He had no wings

to beat the wind that broke
the bough. Down

he came all pink and hollow-boned.
She grieved so far away she couldn't hear

the peeps of hungry squabs that remained.
                        Angels clot like pigeons

on gray-veined markers.
We lace around

the excavated earth and coo
with an antiphon—

"Behold the son that died before his mother,"
the angels choir in a gentle song.

"A boy should never go before his mother,"
we whisper in response, a final psalm.

MISS BLOOM

She dressed like an iris
in purple and green.

Her double-knit pants
clung like shrinkwrap.

She must have loved me.

She offered me goodies
like a kid-eating witch.

Her oven was small
so I never worried.

We sunned on her porch
while I snacked away.

She was Miss Bloom.
Her house was a garden

of knick-knacks and flour
and jello mold sets.

God must have loved her.

He crowned her the queen
of the white picket fence.

Her parlor was garland
with tatted white dahlias,

a doily beneath each objet d'art.
She loved the weeds

as much as the flowers
and gave out blank checks

and supplies for fresh starts.

She played the piano
with a good Christian beat.

We sang like hound dogs;
the high notes were hers.
I must have loved her—

'cause I still hear her voice
when I come to the garden alone.

SUMMERS WITH DANNY AND SUSAN

They appeared each June—libation just before I turned to dust,
two little towhead saviors peering over the station wagon dash

like prairie dogs. Now I think I may have made them up, the aqua
days of pools and riding in Mrs. Winterbottom's mower cart,

through the streets of our new complex, waving like parade grand
        masters
at the denizens of newborn split-levels and crisp ranch-styles

with seedling yards.
                We played among the piles of dirt, weaved between
                the ribs
of skinless houses despite the risk of rusty nails and splintered wood

the builders left behind, until we fell agape into a mound of sand.
The grit was strange against my teeth and ringed my lips in stucco.

If only I had thought to leave some trace among the scaffolds that we
        were
there, tan and ocher like the dancing petroglyphs made by aborigines

who used the very earth to stencil rocks, hardy cliff dwellers
who chewed the loam and spit still life on canyon walls.

THE SWELLS OF SUMMER

It was a sweaty day—
hurray for sunshine

and drenched bodies.
Beneath the wet white shirt,

every muscle speaks
the gospel, every ounce

of fat sings. The lies
are uncovered

that outerwear screened.
The falsehood of coats,

the lying scarf and hat
are put well away.

On that sweaty day,
I uncovered

that I was gay. Poolside,
fathers, sons, brothers,

paraded hairy chests
and muscles. With a trumpet

in my wet white trunks,
I watched them and wondered

then ducked beneath my shirt
and shorts. I could only sink that day.

It was a sweaty day
when I learned to love

the underneath of things.

Beneath my bed, I hid
my Blue Boy magazines.

Beneath my clothes, I hid
my tumescent summering.

TEACHER'S PET

When pain escapes
all at once and splashes
in your face
like the water fountain
in first grade, what can you do
but sit and drip dry?

When letters just won't
take their place like
the little girl next to you
who wanders around
gnarled desks
until the teacher
ties her down
and tapes her mouth,
what is she but
a hostage of knowledge
and a, e, i, o, u,
and sometimes y?

Kay was her name
and I know we shared
special placement
in that teacher's roll book,
and what we learned best
was how to put the "I"
in pain.

LIBBY'S KISS

Her kiss, wet,
her lips like slugs,
but the best
I ever got.

Her legs, thin
as tinker toys,
the wagon wheel joints
her knees—how
could that neck support
her head, a planet
on a straw—
she looked like hunger.

At lunch, the bench
was empty
but for where she sat.
Libby, the idiot
of third grade,
never seen
on swings or slides,
never jumped
the turning ropes.
Eyes rolled
as she walked by.

Kids, cold, hard
as marbles, used her
for their blood raw laughs;
Their corn-fed
anger passed to her
like a hot potato.

I earned her kiss
by being soft.

MAKING IT PERFECT FOR THE BARGE MAN

In the hall, I see your ghost in boxers.
You rise to take antacid every night,

your ephemeral legs bowed as molar roots.
Even when alive, you looked spectral white,

your torso pale, an El Greco nude,
festooned in skivvies faded baby blue.

You packed/unpacked your shaving kit each month
with razors, Barbasol and Prell shampoo.

Six times a year you left to earn our food,
beat your feet on the Mississippi locks.

Mom fretted her nails, spumed her threats,
and cursed the planes that spirited you from us.

Every other month rehearsals met
to practice grieving when you'd leave for good.

MAKE LOVE WITH WAR

If telling Dad I love you
was easy, I'd have hopped

right in that hospital bed with him.
If our hugs had been more snuggle

then shrug, I'd have stroked
his forehead, smoothed his hair

so he'd look polished for the trip.
He and I had rules. I-love-yous

were quick and only said once swords
were sheathed, once unloving deeds

were done. Then affection could
drip from our wounds.

THE DAY DAD DIED

The day Dad died
I had to hitch

a ride   lucky
I had a lover

with a job

except he had
to use my car

The day Dad died
I had to hitch

a ride   lucky
a floor below

my quirky landlady
with golden arched

eyebrows   (compass drawn)
was home   had wheels

and was used to fat
bearded men

weeping   tapping
at her French doors

II

KISSING THE UGLY

Luster
isn't rare. Polish
any nugget and it gleams.
The light reflects, throws jewels
at your eyes, blinds you to the tossing
arm.
     Covet things that eat shine: the scratched
finish, the tree bark—textures that speed bump the
touch, slow caresses down, make careening eyes
stop.
      Who can only glance at Mother Theresa
and not want to linger on her wadded face?
                                          Tip a china cup
to feel the ring of rough where it's severed from the mold.
Burlap seduces the fingers. Go on, fondle the nap.
                                                      Thrill
to stroke a domed belly and meet the interrupt
of navel,
         investigate a bristled chest and trip over
nipples, scratch a hairy back and part
                                       the tufted swirls.
Beauty is quick and thin and bony. Cuddle ugly.

EFFIE MAY'S CONFESSION

The moon was a-howlin' it must be done
and I know it's best to not play chicken.
I always heeds the advice of the sun.

That fool grabbed me, pinned me down. "Time for fun,"
he said. But I ain't got time for messin'.
The moon gets to howlin' if chores ain't done

just right, so it can wax and wane and stun
the night with its sickle of glycerin.
It always heeds the advice of the sun.

Both them globes stroll through time—they never run.
When the corn and peas are fit for cannin',
the moon will be howlin' it must be done.

I pick and pull and hoe until night comes.
I work the dirt until my skin glistens.
Yep, I heeded the advice of the sun.

Its heat was a-tellin' me to steal his gun—
It weren't *my* plan to kill no one, listen,
the moon was a-howlin' it must be done;
he learnt to heed the advice of the sun.

EVIL IAGO, WHO IS SEEN EAVESDROPPING AT THE LEFT

After Othello Relating His Adventures
by Alexandre Cabanal

He's in dark wine, a shade
of lurk, and skulks
behind the marble stairs.

But the jealousy,
you'd think Iago would dress
in the green

that paints a forest, stippled
with pine cones
and layered in moss, a green deeper

than the underbrush.
Othello glows in gold. His sword
foreskinned

in a blue sheath. Desdemona, moon white,
aching to rise
from Brabantio's lap, is tethered

by her father's noble mass—
all merely players
in a French Romantic's universe

bruised dark wine
in the lower left-hand corner.

THE BLUES ARE SOMEONE ELSE'S PAPER CUT

I ride them down no more
to stasis of bone like statuary
to stupor of brain like slow processor
I no longer fall so low

I'm helium high
bounce on life's big belly
fat with laughter
the good times taste like Christmas candy
friends at the door whenever it's opened
I am not alone or blue

I fly
never spread my wings so wide
never muss a feather
I'm neat and spring
flowers and furries
I'm the kind of guy
birds envy when I fly by
never lost or lonely

the blues are someone else's prickly rash
I ride them down no more
to thinning of skin like onion husk
to torpor of spirit like perdition
I don't fall so low

WHILE AT FRISCH'S FOR A TUNA MELT

The servers skitter about the tables
while ladies with leaning towers of hair

led by men with wishbone legs
dodder to the salad bar, hang their canes

around their wrist while dishing out some cole slaw.
My waitress tells the table next to me

that she has cancer,
must have a length of her esophagus removed.

Somehow, this leads into a narrative
of how her earlobe is split because her youngest

pulled an earring through it. Now, she uses Crazy Glue
to close the slit and wear her diamond studs.

On her face, I notice acne scars, healed
but always open—like the counter

at this the watering hole
for those of us who gimp

through life, drop a limb
and just reach down, pick it up,

twine and paste ourselves together
to make it to dessert.

THIRTY-NINE FOR HOT SIZZLE

Black blue highlights bloom
on my edges. Emotional scabs
itch like madness. I can't
keep sane.

I writhe (a burning leaf). His touch
brings welts. I chew my lip.
I judge the anger by the licks—
one for simmer,
thirty-nine for hot sizzle.

I keep a knife under my pillow, hide
the belt, pour out
the liquor. I told the teacher, but
nobody listens.
I can't keep sane.

Did I see Santa peek
through my keyhole?
He saw what we did. He knows
I'm a sinner.

Tonight in my blog, I'll add
my last entry. Dad popped
my cherry. I can't
find his pistol.

III

BREAKFAST OF SOLOMON

Before you augered through the winter crust,
hepatica corralled within your fist,
I watched the yearly running of this scene.
The rutting buck rubbed his horns on bark.
He seemed to love the tree, the youthful green,
unaware that it turns camphire red
before it makes a boney-fingered reach
for God. And through my winter, I rubbed bark.
I threw my arms around a wooden lover
with hopes that I could sand it soft as flesh.
Now you shake me from my hibernation
and in a splurge of warmth, we resurrect
the green. Our red is not the rouge of death.
It's the glow that smithies us together.
We smelt and flow into a single sword
then ache and crave when not in line of sight,
if not near enough to smell the other.
We are new lovers among old friends who
only like to nosh. Roused, fresh and hungry,
from those fleshless nights, we chew each other.
Can you tell your bite from mine? Who spoons
who? What does it matter? In this morning
of us, you splay like a biscuit for me
and lie prepared as I flow over you,
sawmill gravy, into every crevice.

WHAT LINGERS WHEN LIPS PART

After tongue touches tongue, I stagger
backward from the jolt. A spark,
from two juiced wires brushed together,
lights the dark where cobweb belayed bruts
ache to pop their corks.

I try to sober, but trickle quicker
down the treasure trail,
the shortest passage to your tap.
I binge in the cleft of your cellar,
three sheets from a whiff of your oaky vintage.

Your stout arouses taste buds
flaccid from disuse.
Shivers convulse me
days after a taste of your malt brew.

You are a spirit to be quaffed,
not sipped like snobbish cognac.
When I touch your brim to my lip,
your beard is like a margarita's salted rim.

ATLAS ELEGY

for Eric

Your al dente pasta wore a dot of sauce—
a scab atop a capellini swell.
In a cottage cheese container, overnight,
it would gestate in the fridge till you'd free
it from the chilly womb, carry it to work
and warm it in a stranger's microwave.
All our salvaged bowls were friezed with orange
nuked into the molecules of plastic.
When you'd come home, your bleeding knees would keen
from hours of scrubbing other people's tubs;
your hands crazed as the marble floors you'd clean.
At bedtime, you'd anoint yourself with bag balm,
but the sere and fissure of skin advanced.
You became a Doric ruin.

The taste of honest work is salty.
I'd lick it from your neck at night, enjoy
your hairy bulk beneath me, thankful that
disapproving God made Herculean
even queers He couldn't love in daylight.
You shouldered sky and earth apart for me
when my universe was lacking sinew—
when I had no snap back, snap out of it,
snap to it. My limp weight yoked you. I was
the noodle over-cooked, the wet brown bag,
the tag-along on laundry day. You'd wash
the honest work from your clothes and the yawn
from mine. Though double-loaded, you endured.
I, bereft of drive, could only love you.

SAILORS TAKE WARNING

A progression of crags serrates the sky.
The hackles on Earth's humped back prick the clouds
that fester into crying fits. Wind galls
leaves into a swirling panic. The heaving

shoulders of the ocean fret the ships with
sobs that wash the overboard ashore—I
gasp on rising tides and grasp at flotsam
hoping it will bear dead weight. This is grief,

the gale that turns umbrellas inside out.
The rain impales. Miasma curds the air.
Unanchored in the swell, I'm laved away.

Though weeks before he left, I knew he would;
I felt the atmosphere around me churn.
I had prepared, but still, the weather turned.

FIVE YEARS LATER

Remember how I'd hug you from behind
to nuzzle in your hair and then inhale?
Your scent would linger underneath my nose—

a milk mustache. I can't remember how
you smelled—only that you did, only
that the sheets would soak up your aroma,

release your tincture slow for my enjoyment.
Where you once lay, I lie and sniff, try to
suck you back into my life, pull into

my lungs a particle of you as if
there is one left within the weft of cotton.
I would know it, even now. No longer

in my bed or on my lips, you're less than
vapor but more than I can fan away.

MAY DAY

I huddle in a phone booth, ignite
damp tobacco, draw a modest puff

from the half-lit tip, feel
splats pelt my bald spot.

It's like I'm always sick, home
from school, hazed from Nyquil.

My brain drips, my thoughts leak,
and my will floods. Pipes that won't connect

gush a mental blood. The steady drizzle
turns the city gray. Night is coming—

just another cigarette to clear my head.
I wring my hair and lament the cost

of lovers, chew an ink pen cap
into a fray of plastic as I search

the yellow pages. A specialist must exist
for this madness. I hope he is a smoker.

Between inhales, I hear the drip.
I see God's face, brief, in the rolling tendrils

until the winds disperse the holy smoke,
and I know the worst has happened. Then I drop

the cigarette and stamp the devils from the embers.

IV

UNTIL THE RESURRECTION

The chosen among the children
hunting eggs, killing time
until the resurrection.

I must have had the mark
that encouraged such an act—
in the safest of safe places,
on the grounds of this cathedral
where we were flushed with grace.

Sometimes in dreams, you rise
again to wrap your arms around
my waist and lift me from the grass.
Your whiskers rasp my ear, sweat
weeps from your lip, trickles
down my nape. We're prostrate
at the cross.

Sometimes, I wish I wasn't there
to feel the prick of penetration—
the nauseating violence and simultaneous
pleasure of your warmth and forced attention.
I still feel your fervid breath rebuke my neck.

And in the middle of the rape,
I see the watch around your wrist,
the band constricting tufts of hair.
I wonder what time Christ will come;
how long until the resurrection?

A FAT GOLD WATCH

I'm on God's fob chain, not a minute
to myself. I keep watch
in the garden, lay awake
with Christ, toss all night
in the bosom of Abraham.

I kneel for hours watching
the cogs of doctrine turn
the gears of clockwork saints.
God wound
my spring so tight the prayers run

fast. Chimes strike
in my head. The shuddering won't stop.
God synchronized my watch to his,
and now, I can't stop ticking.

ALL THIS AND HEAVEN, TOO

>   Blessed are the cheesemakers
>
>   —*Life of Brian*, Monty Python

    God like a TV
in another room has us
straining to hear above
the drone
        of furnace, the gush
    of plumbing
    the clamor of our brains.

The story is full
of gaps
        and full of
    narrators slapped
off their ass,
        groping the night.
Epistles.
      Commandments.
More Marys than a gay bar.

But, what He holds back
enraptures.

We press our ears
    against the wall.
        Someone says,
   "I think He said, 'stone
thy neighbor,' or was it 'love
    the blasphemer?'"

RELIQUARY SONNET

Imagine how it feels when Lakshmi rides
her glowing lotus through the living room,

think of what it's like when Mother Mary
projects her brilliance straight into your head.

Once the Loa infiltrate, you are snagged.
Their luminescence frays your weft, and you

unravel. Each Celestial grabs a thread and flees.
The unfurling is an itch, deep, entombed.

The rest of life is excavating flesh
to exhume the bones, to cool the prickle

of the most unlikely hallelujah,
lost among the heaps of what God is not.

The digging, it can tear a saint apart—
their tattered pieces, little works of art.

ST. JOSEPH SPEAKS

The wonder of you, corseted by God,
made shapely by who takes the breath away.
A curvature of piety made cup
for seed that sired a rapturous fruit so ripe
it juiced itself. If I could feel your flesh
like beads between my fingers, would it change
my mind that you are only apparition—
a ploy of light and angle to deceive?
Gilded icons, clitorides of hope,
the nerve of mercy pursed behind a fold
that won't recede until rubbed firm by praise.
You have borne a God. Is that not enough?
I watch in awe as you float up to Him,
the only one that knows you're warm inside.

TOWER OF BABEL

Lincoln Logs bring out the Kali in me.
      Tinker Toys, no,
the spindly wooden filigree makes sick
      splintery sounds
like breaking bird bones. (Who could steal their flight?)
      But Lincoln Logs
have heft that dares the hurricane latent
      in creation—
the counterpoint of tongue-and-groove. I'd loom
      above tiny
dwellings I'd assemble, draw back my foot
      with toddler aim
and let manifest the great leveler.
      Back then I knew
the force of gravity prevailed even
      when clad in bun-
ny slippers, that on this earth most things just
      don't rick that neat.
Rarely is there a niche for every bulge.
      Most joists could use
a bit of sistering. Lincoln Logs stack
      plumb alone.

HOW BLAKE RUINED MY SLEEP

I can't help but think there's someone knitting
    in the background.
 I hear the needles click when silence settles
    like my head
on ticking, a feather-floating drift of
    clack-a-clack sounds
muffled by the slipping yarn over blunted
    needle tips.
The frenzied rhythm of creation's
    stitching undermines
the sober tempo of my rest. Where does
    peace live? Not where
there are endless circles pulled through circles—
    curls gripping curls.
Now I'm drifting onto thoughts of woolies
    made from nothing
but a thread of several miles convoluted
    back to warmth
after being treadled thin and useful.
    Some God must be
knitting in the background; otherwise, how
    could we lace so
seamlessly after each unlacing? How,
    little lamb, could
we not unravel after every fleecing?

v

ANIMA COMES ASHORE

> "[…] life is an open sea, she sought to explain
> in sorrow, and to survive women cling to
> the floating debris on the tide"
>
> —*The Astronomer's Wife,* Kay Boyle

    I

Flare, flash
    swim for life
One more storm
    to live through
Lightning takes
    my photograph
    I'm blind

    II

I bob like driftwood
    stripped from
Clash of waves
    I concede another
Limb to sharks
    I'm sore
Don't touch me

Clasping a figurehead
    that floats
When I can't
    I bury my face
In wooden breasts
    and take no chances

In a womb of salt
    my skin molts
    I'm exfoliated

Raking against a coral reef
    I'm exposed
Don't look at me

       III

There's a corset on the beach
Lace it up
    pull tight—no! tighter
    I'm new
    I'm civilized
I can't breathe

ANIMA LAMENTS THE POSSIBILITY OF SEED

To you who knocked me flat
entered me and dropped a seed,
here's the progress report.

You left a gift of numbness
and a curled up boy cringing
in my pelvic cradle.
I can't get past the slippery rocks
to hold him.

He's made of silent tissue that tears
like a wet paper bag
too full of canned goods
or memories that boil a noodle soft.

I won't pump life
into this forced bloom.
I'll uproot him
before the possibility of seed
give him no chance
to pop like milkweed

Sometimes anger flares
my nostrils; I can't find
the verb love. You stole
my N is for nurture, knocked
the wind from my lullaby.
I won't let my blood
feed your issue. I can't wait
to purge
my womb of you.

ANIMA COMMENTS ON ONE NIGHT STANDS

Weight like lead
sinks to the bottom,

a quick descent,
a scream and a fall.

Things get smaller
as they plummet.

The way you placed
your lips on

my cheek
I remember

the light brush
reminding me

I can't fall.
I need a heaviness

from you. Rough me up,
sandpaper me smooth

as percale sheets
then tumble me dry.

You said a word
that sank to my center.

Repeat it please.
Have you ever seen

how fast a rock
will sink in the creek?

That's how I want
to fall in love

and in the morning
I'll make the bed.

ANIMA COMMENTS ON MARRIAGE

When it comes to the point
  of only two bodies   nothing
      but two bodies
We're almost there
   yet not quite lost
in limbs and lips
      hair and hollows

before we fold into one
      another like chocolate chips
  in cookie dough   that instant
before the drop
      down the rabbit hole
      over the waterfall
just a moment after we've
  chugged and panted
      and pushed our
      strand of cars to the apex of
  the track

after we wrench ourselves
  from the claws
that catch   canceled
  gravity   put the kids
to bed

before we've reached
the pinnacle but after I've started
to twist the sheets and
  point my toes
I wonder if
  I put the cat out

ANIMA'S HEADACHE

The moon has my brainstem
knotted   twist-tied   crampy
I have never felt larger
My foot soles are tender
If not for the sun
I'd be slushy   cold as snow cream

Here take my hand
Does the wedding band still play?
No   It's the moon calling fowl

I have no life with you
only last night's meatloaf
cold   greasy
I put it in your lunch   with a note
Do you ever feel the swelling of the moon?

VI

PROLOGUE: ODE TO PROMETHEUS

      O, First Missionary,
you teetered down
the mountain with a spark

in your fennel stalk that rebuked
the squalls of winter, illumed the fissions
in the ribbed earth, and beguiled

the rabbles cowed in the valleys
of death.
      O, First Martyr,
in the chronic abrade of

shackles, does it gall that your
gift begat the gladiator, the sniper,
the arsonist? Was it worth

thirty thousand years
of the eagle's daily nebbing
in your viscera?

      O, First Protector,
the evening when light pierced
the levees of day and rilled

into the lavers of night, a crackling
passion suffused the land
and no dark was left

in which to hide, in which
not to cast the shadow of death—
no rest.

IRENE'S LULLABY FOR A DYING LIGHT

Put down your beakers, Mother.
The earth yawns for you.
Your atoms will be seeds.

I have your x-ray eyes—
I see through your mantle.
So put down your test tubes,

your centrifuge,
your mortar & pestle.
Let go of your atoms. Like seeds

from cottonwood, learn
to drift and be carried.
Put down your reagents,

your scales,
your stirring rods.
Let your atoms scatter, the seeds

of all that you distilled
will sprout without your doting.
Put down your beakers, Mother.
Rest your atoms. Let them go to seed.

DRACULA COURTS HIS NEXT EX-WIFE

Can you hear the mushroom cloud
  of angels choir? They drone for you.
      Look through their swathes, their skin,
to their ichorous veins engorged with nectar.
         Count each blood feather
    while I wipe the spittle
from your chin. I bequeath to you

hunger from the famine in my bones,
  from the dust of Hammurabi's Code,
      the parchment of the Dead Sea Scrolls.
The elements have warped your marrow,
         unswirled your fingertips.
     Remove your spoke from the karmic
wheel and the spark will not decay.

Luminesce, Marie, luminesce! You need
  no sun to melt your wings. The night will wick
      the shimmer from your core, and I will siphon
the blight from your veins. Like the aurora borealis,
        you'll irradiate   at dusk.
    Open a wrist. Part a Red Sea.
Unhinge your jaw, Lover, and feed.

MISS CURIE REGRETS SHE'S
UNABLE TO LUNCH TODAY, MADAME

I will not lay my head upon your chest.
It doesn't help to know your heart's not beating,
Or to dread I will not hear the inspiration
Of organelles and the busywork of
Mitochondria.
                Cells have ceased to port
Your ichor. Platelets have stopped their clamor
Through your veins.
                      The life we had was raucous—
loveDove loveDove loveDove—God's tympani,
Descanted by the chuff of oxygen,
In and out, by murmurs, gurgles and coos.

I bled for you. I thought it was enough
To synchronize my phenotype to yours.
Your lust, a kiss so honed it cuts.
And now, I hate your silent guts.

THE EX-WIFE OF DRACULA COUNTS HER LOSSES.

You, the great cleaver, the splitter of Adam,
what do you care for one small Nobel

prize winner, and why harry me into regretting
that you made all matter scintillate,

set the atomic clock pulsing? I have clambered
atop the lattice of molecules and tallied

electrons, sifted through the hieroglyphs
of periodic law. I know how elements

clot and bleed, how each particle reaches for
another to ballast its listing pivot, to distract it

from its tether. I earned every companion
hailed into my orbit, but you made my life

a lonesome circuit by taking every one.
You pulled us together to pull us apart.

Years ago I called for you, offered sacrifice—
"take me, instead," I pleaded to the hoary sky

while Sophia boiled with typhus and mother's
ribs splintered with each gasping hack. From the window,

Mother, a tuberculoid wisp, watched my sister's
processional as it passed our home. Wearing

Sophia's coat like a woolen ghost, I lagged
behind her slow cortege. Four years later,

I watched as Mother with her last molecule
of mortal coil slashed a cross in the air to bless us,

then wheezed, "I love you," before she deflated and let go.
Next, Pierre, the only one with whom I slept in peace,

kindled the rebirth of hope burnt black, the ashes
out of which myths fly. The sparks he struck

warmed my frozen bones. His throb of moxie
emblazed my veins with paroxysms

that fused our atoms—I did not survive
the sudden cleaving. His heat gone,

his flannel, his tufts of down. Absence nettles
like carbon motes within my bedclothes.

I fan and fan and fan the sheets, smooth them
till the friction burns my palms. But every evening,

I arise black and pitted by the grit of loss,
an evanescing flicker, a lignite smolder,

an ember bedimmed into coal.

THE EX-WIFE OF DRACULA WORRIES AND LIES AWAKE

> Tiefer, tiefer, irgendwo in der tiefe gibt es ein licht
> (Deeper, Deeper, somewhere in the deep there is a light)
>
> —*Hello Earth,* Kate Bush

Have you been eating sheep
again? Babies? Your hunger
unsettles my repose, transfuses

it with cries and bleats.
I have seen you gnaw
on angel bones,

chew on heartwood from the tree
of knowledge, desperate
to get Eden back inside you.

Lucy, Mina, me, our toothsome
necks like honeyed ham,
how many Eves must you consume?

And the Adams that you hide,
what spurious shame to nest
within a fallen man.

In my recurring dream, St. George
gloats above your corpse. Panting
and sweating, he leans

on his sword—your head
a slavering parcel clutched
beneath his arm.

But the face is not your
gauntly angles and planes.
It is globose and fleshy

with the eyes of a sullen
lost boy who declined to clap
for Tinkerbell, who watched

the poison choke her glow,
so he could, like an entomologist,
pin the carcass to a velvet card.

How did I fall into this dankness,
these tossing days abed
in mildewed silk?

I sought to rest
beside the dragons,
unmask the source of lumens

spewing from their paunches.
untangle their atomic leashes,
I bit the apple that smote

Newton. Pierre, my Adam,
built our house on shifting
matter with balsa planks

the slightest force could trample.
His flesh beneath the horses
hooves tattered so easily.

You, mottled but solid,
what carriage could ferry
you from me? And now,

I grope for one that can.
You are like pitchblende,
deep within a spark

that is deadly to distill.

THE EX-WIFE OF DRACULA UNFEELS

Trees concede their cover,
  shake their limbs at the bitter
words the chill whispers
      of what was—
           attention slips.
The cold is still,
  settled. "The breath
is never meant to be seen," I was thinking.
  The snow is unangeled—
undulated like drifts of thought.
  The rubbing, the rubbing,
     but no return of feeling.

THE COUNT TAKES HIS WAKING SLOW

If I could seep into sunset
when sleep kicks me from the nest,
I would not feel so slammed
into twilight.

My arousal has no grace.
It's like righting
a listing obelisk. Pulleys,
ropes and hundreds of slaves
crank open my lid, ratchet me erect.

I rise to the dead language
my bones speak—
the pops, clicks,
cursing from elbows and wrists,
the cackle of hips.
Knuckles reckon back
to when the fist I wag
at God was easy to make.

EX-WIFE OF DRACULA STRUGGLES WITH INDECISION

I have an eternity to touch
       on sore spots and probe
with exsanguinated hands
          all the entrails we have spilled.

Without a second thought,
          I would tumble, brook over bedrock,
until I could make it to the delta,
      to a tropical gulf, and turn
to ash—a holiday without
           the moon-ripened melee.

You cast words that snag
      my skin, clot my viscera.
You spit acid that roots
         in my joints. I recall

      the bloody violence when
you leaned to kiss my neck.
      All night, I trip over replays
  like a hump in the rug.
      I have gone from red to pale—
 I want to settle this right
      now. Should I
  stake your heart or mine?

ACKNOWLEDGMENTS

The author is grateful to these magazines and journals that published the following poems:

"Atlas Elegy" in *Bloom*

"Why I Left the Garden" in *The Louisville Review*

"Libby's Kiss," "Teacher's Pet," and "Until the Resurrection" in *What Goes On*

ABOUT THE AUTHOR

Mark Russell Brown (1963-2011), from Louisville, Kentucky, received his MFA from the Naslund-Mann Graduate School of Writing. His work can be found in *The Louisville Review, BloodLotus, Bloom,* as well as in *Bigger Than They Appear: Anthology of Very Short Poems*. He was a long-standing member of the Green River Writers.

www.ingramcontent.com/pod-product-compliance
Lightning Source LLC
Chambersburg PA
CBHW030159100526
44592CB00009B/362